Snow Leo

By Alison Tibbitts and
Alan Roocroft

PUBLISHED BY
Capstone Press
Mankato, Minnesota USA

CIP
LIBRARY OF CONGRESS CATALOGING IN PUBLICATION DATA

Tibbitts, Alison.
    Snow leopards / by Alison Tibbitts and Alan Roocroft.
        p. cm. -- (Animals, animals, animals)
    Summary: Discusses the physical characteristics, behavior, and life cycle of snow leopards and their current status as an endangered species.

    ISBN 1-56065-106-7
    1. Snow leopard--Juvenile literature. 2. Endangered species--Juvenile literature. [1. Snow leopard. 2. Leopard. 3. Rare animals. 4. Wildlife conservation.] I. Roocroft, Alan. II. Title. III. Series: Tibbitts, Alison. Animals, animals, animals.
    QL737.C23T474   1992
    599.74'428--dc20   92-11447
                                           CIP
                                           AC

Consultant:
John Turner, Lead Keeper
Tiger River Run
Zoological Society of San Diego

Photo Credits:
Alison Tibbitts and Alan Roocroft: Cover, title page, 3, 4, 7, 8, 11, 12, 15, 16, 19, 20, 27, 28, 30, 32, back cover

Zoological Society of San Diego by Ron Garrison: 23, 24

Capstone Press
P.O. Box 669, Mankato, MN, U.S.A. 56002-0669

Air at the top of the world is too cold to breathe. Howling winds churn the snow. A wall of clouds opens for a moment to reveal a ghost. It is really a snow leopard. Haze closes over the cat and he is gone.

Only about two thousand snow leopards live in the wild. This shy animal is so rare that his **species** cannot be counted. Little is known about his daily life. It is difficult to track him. It may take weeks of hiking in the mountains just to see him.

The cat lives in the great mountains of Asia called the Himalayas. The people of Nepal call him "sabu" which means "snow leopard." He likes altitudes between three and four miles high. In summer he may climb farther up to cooler weather.

The snow leopard haunts places below the permanent snow line. His fur colors blend with the rocks around him. This **camouflage** makes him nearly impossible to see. He lies on ledges of cliffs to watch for **prey**. Big trees do not grow at such high altitude. Scrub brush is all there is. So, this animal never learns to be a good tree climber.

A snow leopard is one of the world's most beautiful cats. His icy green eyes have gold flecks in them. He sees six times better than humans do. This ability helps him when he hunts for food.

His paws are big enough for an animal twice his size. The front feet are larger than the back ones. These "snowshoes" keep the cat from sinking down into the snow. Thick pads on the bottoms of his feet prevent him from slipping and sliding. Layers of hair cushion his walk on the rocks.

Snow leopard fur is long and thick. The entire body has **outer hairs** as long as a man's middle finger. Colors range from white to smoky gray. Spots splash in a pattern across the coat. These dark rings have light centers. A woolly **undercoat** traps heat to keep him warm. He looks as though he is wearing a white bib down his chest. Stripes on his forehead look like eyebrows.

The tail is a snow leopard's most amazing body part. This elegant rope is half of the cat's total length. His body and tail are each three feet long. Thick, fluffy hairs cover the tail.

The air is thin and extremely cold where a snow leopard lives. The animal stays healthy because his domed head has special **sinus passages**. Cold air is warmed in these sinuses before it passes to his lungs.

An adult male weighs one hundred and fifty pounds. He stands two feet tall at the shoulder. A female is smaller and weighs close to one hundred pounds. Both have strong shoulder muscles to help them climb steep cliffs.

This animal is the link between great cats and small ones. He is of medium size. He is more like small cats in many ways. He is not a growler. He does not roar like a lion. He makes high-pitched yowls instead. Snow leopards purr. Great cats do not. A whistling chirp is his special greeting.

The snow leopard is always on the move. He finds a new place to rest every day. Early morning and late evening are his most active times. He will travel during the heat of the day. However, he likes cooler hours better.

Most of each day is spent hunting. Surprise is important for success. He may try several times before catching anything. His favorite prey is the mountain sheep called a **bharal**. These sheep live in small groups scattered over a wide area.

A snow leopard hunts alone. He follows a zigzag route across mountain ridges. He travels along the slopes halfway between peaks and valleys. There are fewer prey as the cat climbs higher. He finds the most food in summer months. He crouches low when he hunts on level ground. He seems to disappear into grass and shrubs around him.

This animal is the best jumper in the cat family. He has no trouble dropping down sixty-five feet. From there he leaps onto the back of his prey. He springs fifty feet from ledge to ledge with ease.

A snow leopard lives alone. Each leopard stays a mile away from another leopard even if their territories overlap. Each territory has a fifteen mile boundary. Every cat has favorite places in his area. He follows the same paths again and again. He does so even if he has been away a long time.

The male leopard sprays rocks and trees in his territory. This makes his presence known and tells others his land is claimed. The male and female both scratch marks in sandy soil. They also rake trees with their claws. Somewhere along the way there is a marking post. Cats from all over pass by this special meeting place.

Mating season is the only time when these cats are not alone. A female sprays rocks to alert males. Two or more leopards together are either a mated pair or a mother with cubs. A female's activity pattern changes when she has cubs. She hunts for shorter periods and not so often. She has fewer babies than other cats. This is because there is less food to support the family at high altitudes.

Twin cubs are born in a secure spot every two years. They are helpless for the first six weeks. After that, they chase, romp, and tumble like cats everywhere. The cubs develop climbing skills. They learn to follow their mother over rough terrain. They begin marking territory at about nine months. This is the start toward finding their own area. Cubs stay with the mother for two to three years.

Winter cold drives a hungry animal down into valleys in search of food. A snow leopard goes as low as 4800 feet if prey is scarce. The cat has not learned to be afraid of people. Trouble occurs if he attacks livestock. Angry farmers may kill him and sell his pelt, although this is not legal.

There is still plenty of remote habitat for snow leopards across several Asian countries. But it is being split into small, isolated pockets. Asian peoples are learning about wildlife preserves. These parks are needed if the animals are to survive in the wild.

Over two hundred snow leopards live in zoos. Many have had cubs. These gentle cats get along well with the humans who care for them. This may not be the same as living free in the mountains, but it is a good way to save these beautiful endangered cats from **extinction**.

GLOSSARY / INDEX

Bharal: wild sheep who live high up in the mountains (page 17)

Camouflage: a form of disguise that blends with the background and makes it hard to be seen (page 6)

Extinction: ceasing to exist, no longer living (page 29)

Outer hairs: the coarse, thick hair on the outside of a fur coat (page 10)

Prey: animals hunted and killed by another animal for food (page 6)

Sinus passages: narrow, hollow tunnels in the skull which connect with the nose (page 13)

Species: animals that are alike and can reproduce with each other but not with animals of other species (page 5)

Undercoat: soft layer of thick, short fur growing between the outer hairs and the skin (page 10)

J
599.7442   Tibbitts, Alison   T
Snow Leopards